BOMB THREATS

poems by

MARK ZIMMERMANN

PEBBLEBROOK
PRESS

Published by Pebblebrook Press
PO Box 1271
Wisconsin Rapids, WI 54495

Copy Editor: Signe Jorgenson
Design Editor: Jim Giese

Bomb Threats ©2025 Mark Zimmermann
LC Control Number: 2025917525
ISBN: 979-8-218-74007-8

Printed in the US.

Acknowledgments

Thank you to the editors of the following publications where the poems below previously appeared, some in slightly different form or with slightly different titles:

Bards Against Hunger: Wisconsin Edition: An Anthology of Wisconsin Poets: "Toast"

Bramble: "Inspiration"

Cover Magazine: "Wintergreen"

Cream City Review: "What Happened to Hitler's Mustache"

Ellipsis: "Whores Laughing"

Mobius: The Journal of Social Change: "Bedpans," "Truck Commercials," "Cancer Drug Commercials," "Jessica Mitford, America Still Needs You," and "Bomb Threats"

Nerve Cowboy: "Bedpans" reprint

New Letters: "Coal Pits in the Mountains"

New Verse News: "Exotic Thrills"

Rosebud: "An All-American Game" and "The Hand That Offends"

Stoneboat: "English Conversation, Intermediate Level Units I-III: Emi's and Paul's Homework"

Verse Wisconsin: "Air Show"

Wisconsin Fellowship of Poets Calendar: "Castle Doctrine"

Table of Contents

For Carole—
secret sharer of Joycean pet names

Bedpans

You know what they say about bedpans
—rolling on down production lines,
injection-molded, robot-inspected,
identical thousands every day, stackable
plastic, boxed and bar-coded, expedited
for priority shipment:

The engineer says
Quality design is our promise to you.
The ad man says
From our family to yours.
The hospital owner says
The best in personal care.

As for me,
the days before my father died
I'd pour his urine down the hospital toilet.
Later the itemized bill arrived.
Line 143 said
Male bedpan with low spill adapter: $289.

A one-liter plastic jug, with cap.
Our promise to you
From our family to yours
The best in personal care
$289.
You know what they say about bedpans.

Truck Commercials

The all new, All-American pickup
with military-grade aluminum alloy body.
Not just any truck for any driver.

A master-of-the-frontier wilderness truck
for master-of-the-frontier wilderness men
fording stream, ascending hill, challenging
every rocky terrain, scaling mountains
to survey pristine valleys below,
flying through the air in slow, slow motion,
caked in mud to show who's unstoppable,
storming the rugged, untouched land.

Blaze through forests in an unpaved world, O truck
and military-grade driver—a world
without women, without any traffic,
no cities or smog, no gridlock or death,
no stoplights or limits of any kind,
no sprawling concrete acreage of freeways,
O truck for a free and manly America
of simple truths and military-grade aluminum alloy bodies.

Who in that world would need to consider
the fine print of cash back and 0% APR financing,
not to mention the oil fields of the Middle East?

Gutsy pioneers, rugged individualists, nobody's fools
taking it straight from the assembly line,
Madison Avenue calls them to duty.

Whores Laughing

The drunk pimps at the bar
all agree:

There's a practiced laugh
that whores let out
john by john by the thousands

—a laugh that laughs
needing the cash, coming on worn
with a knowing, fuck-all air.

Have you ever heard it?

The Hand That Offends

Cut off and thrown in the river
it floated out to sea.

The one-handed people waved goodbye,
the two-handed people stared.

Then they buried a glove
with the name of the hand
and looked out over the sea.

There went the shark fin thumb,
roving and rising hand.

It found a new home, threw a stone.
Nights it fingers the braille of starlight.

Castle Doctrine

John Wisconsin here
Reporting for duty
To defend our freedom
Protect us all
Guard against tyranny
Serve our nation
And God above.

Besieged and surrounded
By murderers and thieves
I'll charge forth
Guns drawn
Save the innocent
Kill all the scum.

Having won the day
I'll holster my tools
Seek nothing for myself
Decline all interviews
Return to normal life
Just doing my job.

The key to the city
Lead car in the parade
The adoring children
The Governor's phone call
The grateful headlines
I'd never ask for any of that.

English Conversation, Intermediate Level Units I-II: Emi and Paul Watch the NFL

Emi and Paul are second-year students at an international school in Tokyo. Lately Emi has been watching American football on TV because sports are a great way to learn about different cultures. Today she has invited Paul to watch a game with her. Let's gather around the TV and speak English with Emi and Paul!

I. Very Close Friends

Look, Emi! Jets are flying toward the football stadium!

I see them, Paul. They are F-22 fighter-bombers.

Why are they flying toward the stadium?

The jets are flying toward the stadium, Paul, because NFL owners and American military leaders are very close friends.

You and I are close friends too, Emi.

Yes, Paul. You and I are very close friends, but not as close as NFL owners and American military leaders.

People in the stadium are standing up and cheering for the F-22s now, Emi. Everyone seems very friendly.

That's right, Paul. The people are giving the F-22s a warm welcome.

Are the jets returning from a bombing mission?

No, Paul. At NFL games, the jets fly only to entertain their NFL friends.

But America is at war, isn't it, Emi?

America has been at war for our entire lives, Paul.

War makes me afraid, Emi. Does war make you afraid, too?

Yes, it does. Thousands of children like us are dying in wars.

Emi?

Yes, Paul?

Do you think we will die in a war?

I don't know, Paul. I hope not.

I <u>am glad that</u> we are close friends, Emi.

I <u>also am glad that</u> we are close friends, Paul.

II. A Very Special Occasion

The F-22s have flown away now, Emi.

Yes they have, Paul. Soon the game will begin.

What are all those people in the stadium wearing on their heads, Emi?

I don't know, Paul. It looks like they are large triangles made from yellow foam plastic.

I have never seen hats like that before, Emi.

Neither have I, Paul. This must be a very special occasion.

Why do you think that?

Because, Paul, all the people removed their hats and stood up to sing at the same time, then they all waved their hats in the air and cheered when the F-22s flew over the stadium.

And when the singing was over, Emi, and the F-22s were gone, all the people sat down and put their special hats back on at the same time!

Good point, Paul! I almost forgot that.

Many of the people wearing the special hats are also drinking beer from very large cups, Emi.

In some cultures, Paul, beer is a sacred beverage. And I have heard that in America Sunday is a sacred day.

We can learn a lot about other cultures by watching TV, Emi.

Yes we can, Paul.

Air Show

The first roar bolts from nowhere. Like a flashback, flinch
and duck before the bomb hits. When F-16s gun it
diving in low, high-rise windows shudder in their frames,
cats race to cower under beds, and the toddler
two shaken floors up wails in witless terror
as over and over the jets roar, just for show. Lucky girl,
she knows only thunder, not the fire that names
air raids on cities where other people live
or lived. Lucky she's not collateral burned alive—
not when Milwaukee's air show returns for summer
fun at the beach, for the oohs and ahhs of an afternoon
parade of family-friendly air power. Outside
not one bird's in flight, no robin or crow.
The crowd overflows.

The Dachshund (Paranormal Grief)

I guess it was how I was feeling about my father.
—Niklas Frank

Hans Frank, Governor General
of Poland, 1939–45—tried, convicted,
hanged at Nuremberg—

his sister touted reincarnation.
His widow and children opted for séance.
Nothing happened

till little Niklas, not yet nine, imagined
the neighbor's dachshund
possessed his father's soul.

Niklas talked to that dachshund
for two long weeks, hoping
the dog would impart

a father-to-son revelation.
Nothing happened
so he strapped the dog with explosives and blew him up.

Toast

I own the world's most expensive toaster
—a platinum-plated DeLuxury classic,
a gem-studded wonder of eight-slice art.
My housekeepers buff it each Sunday.

Uptown at the annual Society Faire
we toaster cognoscenti nod, brunching
while knowing our taste enriches
the world far beyond our toaster salon.

For as there are breadlines of daily need
(not everyone can buy a toaster)
we pledge surplus bread to the pantries of the world
providing toast to the wretched poor.

Each noonday I savor
the staff of solidarity, served
with butter and marmalade:
O crispy philanthropic delight!

F-bomb Sonnet

Sonneteers' metric obscenities
(do yourself impossibilities)
bring Reverend Pratt to his good knees
beseeching poets: *O Judas Priest!*—
keep writing sonnets filthy as these
and the devil himself will come squeeze
you in the privates until you seize
up and howl like rabid chimpanzees
typing out Hamlet soliloquies
bemoaning hellish conspiracies'
unspeakably naked heresies
akin to the blackguard ecstasies
begetting rank venerealees
who reek like your crappy similes!

Allegory With Ball

Crowds wait long in line to see
a ball behind velvet ropes.

Not just any ball.
The game ball.

Under shatter-proof glass
with laser optic motion sensors,
armed guard on duty.

The ball was thrown, then caught.
Men ran, then signed their names to it.

Ticker tape awaited the victors.
Soon the president would call.

Headlines declared
Historic Victory!

Learn from the past,
eye on the ball.

Powell

I saw the best Boog of any generation destroy the ball,
     hammering hysterical taters—going
going... gone! over the fence into angry Yankee Mudville streets,
Boog
who clipped the hippest Angel pitchers' wings, torquing imported
     fastballs by Louisville
          connection c-r-r-rack, rawhide hissing into waves of
          transcontinental night, Boog
who dreamed of hot dogs in the dugout, who sent hollow-eyed
     hurlers to cold water showers—moonshots floating across the
     tops of cities—soon
          contemplating Boog from the minor leagues, Boog
who psyched out hurlers in enemy bullpens and saw
     unshaven stunned closers
          staggering on mounds illuminated, seraphim who blew
          the three-run lead with sweaty eyeballs hallucinating
          Boog's grand slam and insane tragedy of waivers;
who got tossed by the ump for ranting and crazy obscene
     gestures while Boog trotted around first,
who cowered naked in locker-rooms, no women allowed, burning
     Boog baseball cards in wastebaskets,
          chewing that awful Topps gum, listening to The Big Game
          through roaring coliseum walls of AM transistor radio,
who got their pubic bells rung in bush league Laredo by
     screaming line drives
          Boog hit all the way from Baltimore, brain-throbbing agony
          beneath the codpiece of the skull,
who dreamed of chin music in Greyhound buses, who vanished
     in Poughkeepsie or Peoria
          with purgatoried dreams, nightmare of bobble-head Oriole doll,
          spitball and Amerika and endless Boog...

What Happened to Hitler's Mustache

Already the Russians marched through Berlin so I deserted my guard post deep in the bunker and shaved the dead Führer with a straight-edge blade. Rigor mortis had not yet claimed his upper lip. In the next room Bormann plotted against Himmler and Göring. Artillery shook the walls. Working quickly, I packed the whiskers in a meerschaum locket, lugged the corpse upstairs, set it ablaze, and fled on foot for Spain, evading vengeful night-search parties and the light of the too-near moon.

What little I owned the war had destroyed. Hitler's mustache was my sole asset, one I was ready to fight for had the need arisen. To certain collectors it might have been as valuable as a Napoleonic forelock or a sliver of the True Cross—so long as I concealed the depth of my poverty from any prospective buyer. Lacking the proper connections, however, I began my journey with only cautious hopes.

Opportunities for concealment presented themselves. By daylight I slummed in abandoned bomb shelters, half-sunk barges, coal bins, anywhere quiet. After dusk I might barter a few of the longer whiskers for peasants' tobacco scraps, boar meat, or slabs of black-market cheese.

Yet before and beyond the Spanish border the ideal collector eluded me. My locket's hair treasure dwindled by the day. Nearly broke in Barcelona, I bound the remaining whiskers into a paint-brush tip that I sold to a portrait hack who did up the tourists in the middle of town. He paid me off in cheap wine.

I drank it down, then stepped back to watch him paint. Under his brush the tourists' moles, warts, and scars shrank or disappeared. Many applauded his technique. Then they paid for the distorted faces they took quite happily home.

Sleepwalkers With Guns

Cigarettes don't kill
people, lung cancer kills people.

Drunk driving doesn't kill
people, car crashes kill people.

Opioids don't kill
people, overdoses kill people.

Sleepwalking off a cliff doesn't kill
people, hitting bottom kills people.

Wake up!

Omnivore

Digest the predator.
Spit out the prey.

Poem

Clowns have taken over the morgue
—autopsy-turvy!

Wintergreen

One star-blue pillow mint. November breeze,
    her dreamed hair.
We lay beneath the window that waters the night sky.

No troubadour's velvet shawl our love
like the severed hands of thieves
        folded in prayer.

Not only so many years ago, not only
years. Not only rain swept our dunes
into the sea

so far gone we were beautiful

An All-American Game

Emily Dickinson takes the field
as if to sing the national anthem
at the World Series.

Ladies and gentlemen
rise, observe her silence,
hands over hearts.

An outsize flag waves
across the outfield,
full color guard saluting.

Instead of our rockets and red glare,
though, the poet cries out
I heard a Fly buzz—when I died...

As the crowd sings along
a fly big as a fighter jet roars
overhead, swoops in

like an eagle,
carries flag and color guard away.
The umpire dusts home plate.

When the King be witnessed...
—see to see—
Emily Dickinson heads home.

Coal Pits in the Mountains

The first night we got drunk
we drank Radevsky's Ripple wine.
By firelight on the riverbank
we dared each other to be a man

so Radevsky skinned a dead rat,
smoked ten Chesterfields at once
and chugged a cupful of piss.
None of us dared beat that.

Instead we paused, began to deride
what older men tried or knew:
fatherhood, coal mining, suicide.
Radevsky did those things, too.

Talking to Cancer *(Cancer Talks Back)*

What might I say to this newfound tumor?
"I want you to die"? Suppose it'd say
Now don't you be such a gloom-and-doomer

as if I'd conjured black magic humor:
Abracadabra. You vanish—away!
What could I say if that newfound tumor

continued: *Fossil-fueled baby boomer,*
we were born to live large. Such is our age
so don't you be such a gloom-and-doomer;

you're but a resource, I'm the consumer.
Our sun always shines, our climate won't change.
What could I say to that newfound tumor?

Shrinking it would restore health much sooner.
Better yet, kill it!   *O tsk tsk, rage, rage,*
now don't you be such a gloom-and-doomer.

Some growths are benign, not this rank bloomer
—a Marlboro Man at home on the range.
What could I say to this newfound tumor?
Now don't you be such a gloom-and-doomer.

Classic Rock Radio

I hope I die before I get old.
—The Who

Take me home tonight, forever
young, feel so right, rock 'n roll
rebel, rebel nation, revolution,
teen sensation. Replay the roles
from forty, fifty years ago.

Let it be. Let it go. Turn it up
and catch a ride. Rock 'n roll
will never die. Shake this town,
burn the house down and blow.
When one left early from the show

the band played on to light a pyre,
drove the devil's highway higher—
high as the heedless youngblood highs
where all those rockin' reelings flowed.

From forty, fifty years ago
till coming down to no surprise
that funeral homes now advertise
on classic rock 'n roll radio,
where the hits keep coming till you go.

Here comes rock eternity,
up in smoke, commercial-free.

Back in black.
Don't look back.

It's only rock 'n roll radio.

Godzilla vs. the First Robin of Spring

King of the Monsters!
State Bird of Wisconsin!

Godzilla breathes fire and trashes nations.
Robin chirps and splashes in birdbath.

Godzilla wipes out the military.
Robin flies north as the planet warms.

Godzilla fries all pride to ash.
Robin feels the heat rise each year.

Godzilla warns of folly and extinction.
Robin descended from dinosaurs.

See "American robins now migrate 12 days earlier than in 1994."
State of the Planet, Columbia University (April 2020),
https://blogs.ei.columbia.edu/2020/04/01/robins-migrate-
12-days-earlier/

Exotic Thrills

Luxury shooting ranges
dot the tourist colony of Guam,
draw planeloads of Japanese.

They want an authentic
American experience
unavailable at home:

blasting away with firearms.
Pistol, shotgun, M16,
submachine gun—open fire,
get a glossy souvenir photo.

Their moment of exotic thrills
over, the tourists return
to life in Japan.

Where in 2017
there were three
gun homicides.

Inspiration

As if blue lightning were discovered
alive at the bottom of the sea.

As if a golden ratio flowed
from islands at the vanishing point.

As if there were a vanishing point.
As if Death's flag will never touch the ground.

Old Canes

Not the old canes
huddled and bucketed
in shuttered pawnshops

but older canes
out for a stroll
after their users die.

Canes
that know
they got the job done.

Canes that unscrew
their dented caps
and mock the Sphinx,

dancing with Ahab's leg
while chugging
down the hooch.

Thirsty old canes
giving the finger
to Cousin Nightstick.

Born in the woodland
canes—shadowing
question marks,

getting it on
with witchy broomsticks.
Invisibilia's canes.

Tapping out time behind
the boathouse, whispering
names marked for departure.

Spellbound
castaway
canes.

Schadenfreude

I may as well admit it:
I have taken and continue to take
pleasure in certain extreme misfortunes.

Not the old, enduring cruelties
—fire and flood, famine, war—
that routinely strike so many down,

though I'll own up to chuckling
when a texting driver goes over the cliff
or an anti-vaxxer dies of Covid.

Sometimes I even wish I'd dreamed up the Darwin Awards:
So long, idiot—you had it coming!

I also know by common standards
something is badly wrong in the heart
when moral judgement partners with malice.

True as that is, I doubt there'll ever be
a shortage of actors for schadenfreude
or its grubby one-act morality plays.

The ever repetitive plots never change
 yet I can't quite give them up, it seems.
How about you?

Mona Lisa Postcard

Saw the Mona Lisa at the Louvre
—what a disappointment.

Long lines, wall-to-wall crowd,
serpentine velvet cordons winding,
thousands herded and corralled
on our inching pilgrimage to the queen.

Up close at last she seemed
more distant than ever,
a guarded specimen cased in glass.

As if to salvage the moment
I bought a postcard on the way out.

Over the years
that cheap, touristy knock-off
has given me more enjoyment
than the priceless original ever did.

Taped to the fridge door
it'll catch my eye,
once in a quiet while conveying
a semblance of Mona Lisa mystique
that draws me in.

That old postcard has left me wondering
more than once: If
ever back in Paris, maybe
try to see Mona Lisa again?

Poem group begins in just a few hours...

and I have no poem to bring.

I've been trying for days to get something started
with "a pancake on an ironing board"
but that line's gone nowhere.

I've also had the phrase
"a monocle for Cyclops"
floating around in my head
but that's been a non-starter too.

It's good to know that if someone shows up
at our poem group without a poem,
they are always welcome
at the poetry table, no questions asked.

One can easily imagine a parallel universe
where our poem group is an evil and sadistic poem gang
that scorns and torments those who show up
without poems.

In a happier parallel universe
a poet without a poem might inspire the group
to launch a week-long Roman orgy
revelling in bawdy old odes and panegyrics
as a form of compensation.

So many universes, so many poem groups.

Perhaps it is best to stay in this world
and in this earthly poem group
even if all one has to start with
is a pancake on an ironing board
and a monocle for Cyclops.

The Rumors

Word around campus had it I died.

A department colleague told me this
after I got out of the hospital.

Someone must have heard one thing
then passed it on as another.
Tales of the afterlife have spread from less.

And yet the news brought a rush
as if I'd accomplished something great
or had proved an old adversary wrong.

Such a rumor was, after all,
the next best thing to rising from the dead.

I imagined Mark Twain dropping by to visit:
Congratulations! Have a cigar.

Later I wondered how long till the day
my rumor will have its final glory.

Age-old beliefs and their rumors await.

Tomorrow

Tomorrow I plan to write nothing.
No poetry, no prose,
not so much as a to-do list for the freezer door.
I need a break from routine.

By tomorrow I mean one day only,
not an open-ended future time.

So if tomorrow I happen to die
this poem becomes far more poetic than I intended.

Or maybe tomorrow I change my mind
and start writing what becomes my best poem ever.
Then today's poem won't have much of a future.

Some people write every day, good for them.
I write almost every day
but tomorrow I plan to write nothing.

The Cycle

New laptops for the tech school faculty arrive
on a day widely and warmly greeted
as a Day of Progress

Progress meaning
among other things—out with the old laptops

old laptops meaning
those that were new two years ago.

Soon they will be packed off
like those they replaced two years ago
were packed off
to schools in need in lands once ruled
by colonizers not so different
than the billionaires now running Silicon Valley.

Hand-me-downs are not the end
or the final write-off
of the high-tech cycle.
Recycling is

recycling often meaning
the rich dump toxic waste on the poor.
Extract rare earths, extract heavy metals
from laptop scrap,
poison the earth and sicken
animal and plant alike.

The cycle consumes and continues:
On the day the faculty's laptops arrive,
the model to replace them is already waiting.

English Conversation, Intermediate Level Units III-V: Emi's and Paul's Homework

Emi and Paul are still second-year middle school students in Tokyo. They like school very much. One day they would like to visit America. Let's speak English with Emi and Paul!

III.

Who is that lady on your smartphone, Emi?

That lady on my smartphone is Kathy Griffin, Paul.

Who is Kathy Griffin and what is she doing?

She is a comedian who is explaining her picture of Donald Trump beheaded.

What does beheaded mean, Emi?

Beheaded was part of our English vocabulary for today, Paul. Did you not do your homework?

No, I did not do my homework, Emi. Please don't tell the teacher.

I will not tell the teacher, Paul. I will help you do your homework.

Thank you very much, Emi.

You're very welcome, Paul.

IV.

Where <u>should we do</u> our homework, Emi?

I don't know, Paul. But <u>we should do</u> our homework.

Let's go to the ice cream shop!

That is a <u>very good</u> idea, Paul. Let's go to the ice cream shop. I like ice cream <u>very much</u>.

<u>My favorite flavor is</u> vanilla fudge, Emi. <u>Is your favorite flavor</u> vanilla fudge?

No, Paul. Vanilla fudge <u>is not my favorite flavor.</u> I like butter pecan.

I will buy you a <u>double scoop</u> of butter pecan, Emi, <u>if you tell me</u> what beheaded means.

Thank you very much, Paul. Beheaded means a head has been <u>removed from</u> a body, <u>usually by</u> cutting with a sharp object.

Sharp is the opposite of dull, <u>isn't it</u>, Emi?

Yes it is, Paul.

V.

Ice cream comes from cows because ice cream is made from milk, Emi.

That's right, Paul. It's why ice cream is so delicious.

Was your double scoop of butter pecan delicious, Emi?

Yes, Paul, my double scoop of butter pecan was delicious. I liked it very much.

Do you also like Kathy Griffin very much, Emi?

I have never met Kathy Griffin, Paul.

Look, Emi! Isn't that her over there at the ice cream counter?

No, Paul. Over there is someone who looks just like her.

How do you know that someone who looks just like Kathy Griffin is not Kathy Griffin, Emi?

I know because these days she always comes to ice cream shops with a bodyguard, Paul.

These days Kathy Griffin never comes to ice cream shops without a bodyguard, Emi?

Yes, Paul. That's right.

Cancer Drug Commercials

What an ideal summer day
for fresh air and recreation
in the great American outdoors.

See those people cavorting
beneath a blue sky,
soaking up the warm sun,
breathing in the dreamy air?

They are the healthiest-looking citizens
in all of Pharmatopia

strolling through the green,
playing fetch with the family dog,
gathering round the picnic bench.
The answer to hopes and prayers
available for a price.

Occasional side effects
—bankruptcy
eviction
hunger
suicide—
have been reported.

There is no doctor to call
in the sunless back alley
where Wall Street and Madison Avenue meet.

Jessica Mitford, America Still Needs You

The funeral home down the road
now employs a dog to help
ease the pain of bereavement.

Lately this friendly fellow's been starring
in TV ads unfailingly aimed
at all but the hardest hearts.

There he goes
in soft focus and slow motion,
crossing a green field
while an unseen narrator pledges
to all a dignified parting.

We are told
the dog will attend these farewells
and gently comfort the dearly beloved.

We are not told
that first one must pay
ten grand or more

to have the corpse gutted,
pumped full of toxins, and boxed
before the dog eases any bereavement.

Yesterday I saw him
out in the parking lot,
mounting a bulldog
behind a hearse
as if to say
Fuck this business.

Bomb Threats

Making a bomb threat used to be so easy.

Thousands and thousands of public phones
were scattered across America.

Just slip
into booth,
put cloth
over mouth,
call in
and be gone
before anyone knew.

But those were the old days.

Privacy and undetected movement
are becoming things of the past.
Anyone can be tracked anywhere now.

Instant GPS tracing.
Constant satellite tracking.
Voice recognition software.
Police cams everywhere.
Facial recognition AI's
racial profiles, programmed eyes.

Where does it all end?

Though getting away with a bomb threat today
is no longer so easy for some,
it's easy as ever for others

—those who command the missiles and jets,
who publicly announce
all options are on the table.

But listen to them complain
if a bomb threat ever comes their way.

Lucky for them so many people believe
the pen is mightier than the bomb.

Max's Bird

That spritely, blue and yellow macaw
         squawking and swinging
on a perch
            outside the cage
hung from the ceiling years ago,
how many times I've recalled it
since the day Jorgen took me to Max's flat.

What a fine bird.
Was it at peace in captivity?
Given an open window, would it fly?
I wondered what it thought of humans.
I wished I could speak its language.

Not that it matters now.
Last week it all came out
from a long-lost photo and a call to Jorgen.
Max never had a bird.

Max never had a bird—I say it, think it, know it now.
Still the truth seems off.

From where did this wing of false memory fall?
Since when did it nest in my head?
Every plume, quill, and squawk a fiction,
figments of a life unlived
yet still I "remember" that bird
and see it as before.

What else in my mind may never have happened?
In falsehood or forgetting, I wonder what's next.
Maybe I am ill.

But part of me is glad Max had no bird.

I imagine a parrot soaring
in daily free flight over the forest,
a never-caged guardian of egg.

One way or another that bird is real.

The Teacher

Back when Hirohito was worshipped as a god,
the teacher who ran through the burning school
to rescue the emperor's photograph
but perished in the attempt—she was hailed
as a paragon of bravery and deepest devotion
more beautiful than life itself.

Most Japanese and others I've asked
believe the teacher was badly misguided,
a fanatic who died for nothing,
and I have only rarely questioned
their values or their views.

In grayer moments, though,
I pause:
So that is what it is like to believe,
to really believe and be committed
to all-out sacrifice, a selfless end.

I have had an easy life.
I've never had to risk it all
for anyone or anything. So far
the burning building has always been elsewhere,
the person in peril never near.

I sometimes imagine
the teacher's voice
calling out across our lives:

If ever your moment of crisis arrives,
will you have what it takes
to follow me into the flames?

Author Bio

Mark Zimmermann's poems have appeared in a variety of venues: the Madison Museum of Contemporary Art, Milwaukee Public Radio's *Lake Effect* program, *Rosebud, Cream City Review, New Letters, Mobius: The Journal of Social Change*, and elsewhere. His first poetry collection, *Impersonations*, was published by Pebblebrook Press in 2015. Currently he is finishing a poetry manuscript, working title *Why Not Write Your Name Like This?*, centered on his time living in Japan from 1990-2001. He lives in Milwaukee with his wife Carole and their cat Katinka.